The Unholy Book of Litanies:
Liturgy For The Devoted & Damned

By Walter Red

Secular Hardcover Edition
...Ghost Written • Self-Forged • SFD • Still Here...

Copyright © 2025 Walter Red Books

All rights reserved. No part of this publication may be reproduced, distributed, or transmitted in any form or by any means, including photocopying, recording, or other electronic or mechanical methods, without the prior written permission of the publisher, except in the case of brief quotations embodied in critical reviews and certain other noncommercial uses permitted by copyright law.

This is a work of poetic fiction and memoir. Names, characters, places, and incidents are either the product of the author's imagination or used symbolically. Any resemblance to actual persons, living or dead, is purely coincidental or allegorical.

Cover design, interior layout, and branding by Walter Red. Some content was developed using advanced AI-assisted creative tools under authorial supervision.

Printed in the United States of America.

ISBN: 979-8-9995172-0-3

For more information, visit:
www.walterredbooks.com

From the Ashes, To the Flame

To everyone who left
I forgive you.

Not because it was okay --
But because I can't carry this weight
and still hold a pen.

This wasn't about revenge,
It was about resurrection.

I loved you.
Even when I shouldn't have.
Even when it hurt.

Thank you for breaking me
Because now I know how to rebuild.

I survived.

"Almost all people have this potential for evil, which would be unleashed only under certain dangerous social circumstances."

--Iris Chang, The Rape of Nanking: The Forgotten Holocaust of World War II

邪悪な失恋詩集

"Man is an animal who has to live a lie in order to live at all."

— Ernest Becker, Escape from Evil

Imprecations & Blasphemous Exhumations
The Book Of Fire

Wound I: Anathema

LITANY I: THE SEARCH
LITANY II: THE HUNT
LITANY III: THE JOURNEY
LITANY IV: THE BINDING
LITANY V: THE CONSUMING
LITANY VI: THE DEVOTION
LITANY VII: THE VESSEL
LITANY VIII: THE INITIATION

Wound II: Execration

LITANY IX: THE BODY
LITANY X: THE PRAYER
LITANY XI: THE CRAVING
LITANY XII: THE SPIRAL
LITANY XIII: THE CONFESSION
LITANY XIV: THE ALTAR
LITANY XV: THE WORSHIP
LITANY XVI: THE SACRIFICE

Wound III: Malediction

LITANY XVII: THE RITUAL
LITANY XVIII: THE FORGIVENESS
LITANY XIX: THE ANOINTING
LITANY XX: THE ASCENT
LITANY XXI: THE COLLAPSE
LITANY XXII: THE MEMORY
LITANY XXIII: THE RESURRECTION
[REDACTED]

The Book Of Ash

The Confessional Pages
Shrine Room
Watchers Gloss
Devotional Index
Concordance of the Wounds

Yellowfield

The Gate Before the Orchard

PRELUDE

"Writing about the unholy is one way to confront the holy."

-Clive Barker

Non benedictus.

Sed vivit.

This is the seal they could not break.

The book was unblessed.
But it survived anyway.

THE BOOK OF FIRE

Wound I:

ANATHEMA

(THE CAST-OUT)

THEY DID NOT CHOOSE YOU.
SO YOU BECAME THE VOICE THAT NEVER FALTERED.

Litany I-VIII:
The First Descent

ANATHEMA

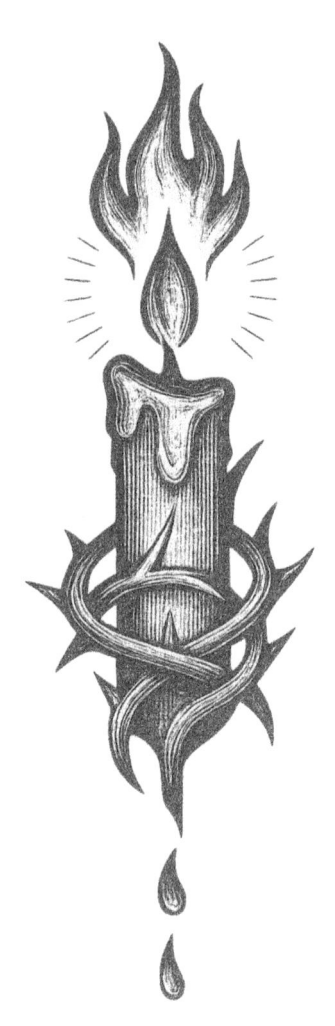

First Recorded: MMXIC, Last Invocation: Unknown

The Word That Was Never Said
(The Search)

I wasn't born with language.
I was born with reaction.

A clenched jaw. A wince.
A look away when it got too tender.

So when they asked me what I wanted –
I didn't say "love"
I said nothing.

This is not a story.
this is what leaked through the cracks.

These are not poems.

These are litanies —
recited until the silence changed shape.

Call it prayer.
Call it penance.
Call it what I couldn't at the time.

Begin with the word you never said.
Say it now. Out loud.
(Yes, even if it's their name.)

"This litany is spoken on burnt soil."

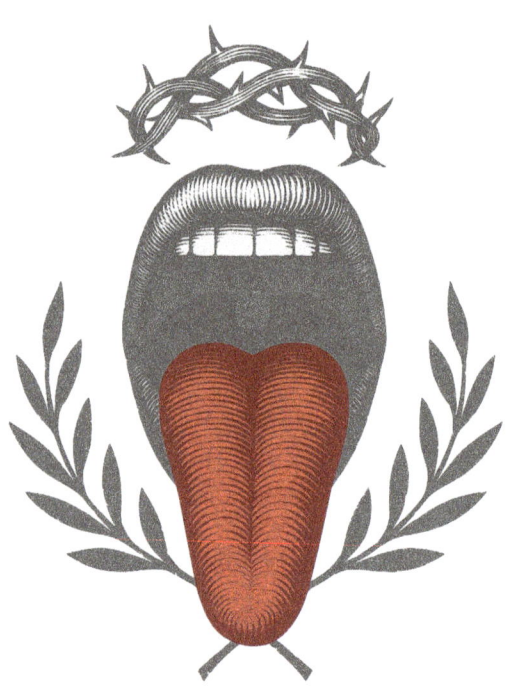

Blueprints of a Bruise
(The Hunt)

You saw my bruise and called it a blueprint.
Not for pain, But for design.

You said the pattern was familiar.
As if you had read my ache before — etched into leather,
Pinned between skin and memory.

You kissed it like scripture,
Tongue tasting the history
Of every failed father
That carved me hollow.

Your hands spoke in fists,
And I opened like scripture
Beneath a pulpit of sweat.

I was not afraid, I was ready.

To be read.
To be rewritten.
To be reformed.

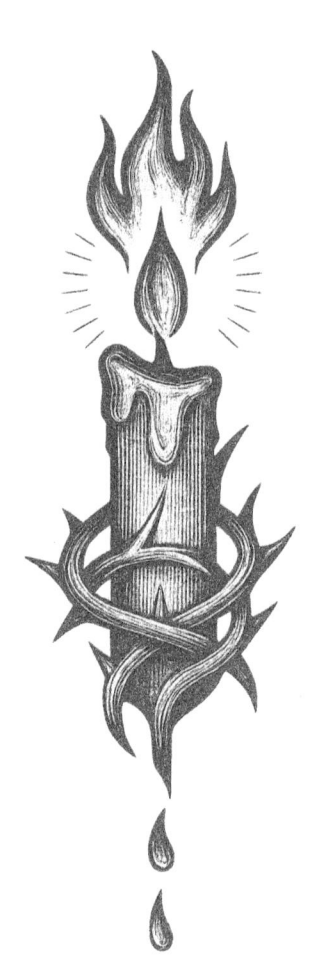

Kneeling Is Not Consent

(The Journey)

I knelt, Not for permission—
But to remember. The shape of you above me,
The gravity of your hips,
The psalms pressed into my neck.

Your belt buckle was a gospel.
The zipper a sacrament.
The moment of entry a holy reckoning.

And I — your altar.

I burned for your hands,
Cupped around the fragile shell
Of my resurrection

Every thrust, A litany.

Every breath, A hymn.

I carried you like a relic, Inside my chapel of ruin,
Lit only by the stained-glass memory
Of what we never became.

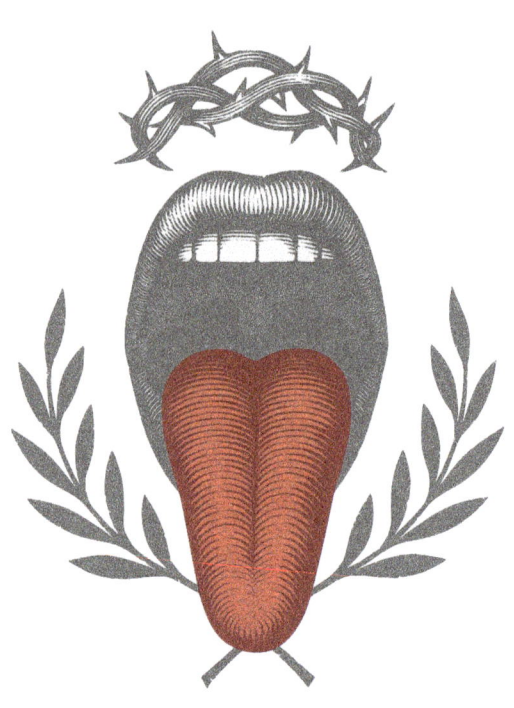

Beads and Bite Marks

(The Binding)

He tied my wrists with a rosary,
Looped not for prayer,
But for permanence.

Each bead a memory,
Each knot a silence I was forced to carry.

He whispered commandments into my ear
That I broke on purpose.

And when he struck me,
I felt baptized.

Not by water,
But by want.

I was scripture unspooling.

And in his hands,
I became both bondage and believer.

Eaten Alive, Thank You
(The Consuming)

I asked him to devour me slowly,
but he came hungry,
teeth first.

He chewed through the parts of me I had left unnamed.
There was no tenderness in his mercy.

Only breath —
hot and jagged —
on the rim of my undoing.

He sucked my spirit from its sheath
And swallowed.

And I thanked him for the privilege
Of becoming pulp

In the mouth of a monster
I mistook for a messiah.

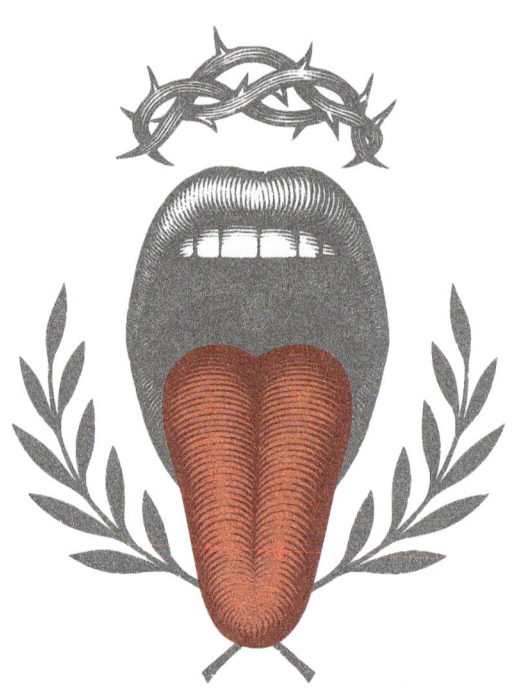

Praise with a Mouthful

(The Devotion)

Every night I made my altar at his feet –
Naked but for the shame
He draped across my shoulders like velvet.

I learned to say thank you with my mouth full.

I kissed the ground he walked on,
Even when it burned.

He never asked me to worship.

He simply stood there –
Beautiful and unrepentant –

And I bowed anyway.

Chalice Cracked, Still Thirsty
(The Vessel)

He poured himself into me like wine
Into a chalice too chipped to hold grace.

I leaked.
He laughed.

And still he filled me again.

Not because I was worthy.
But because I was empty enough to contain him.

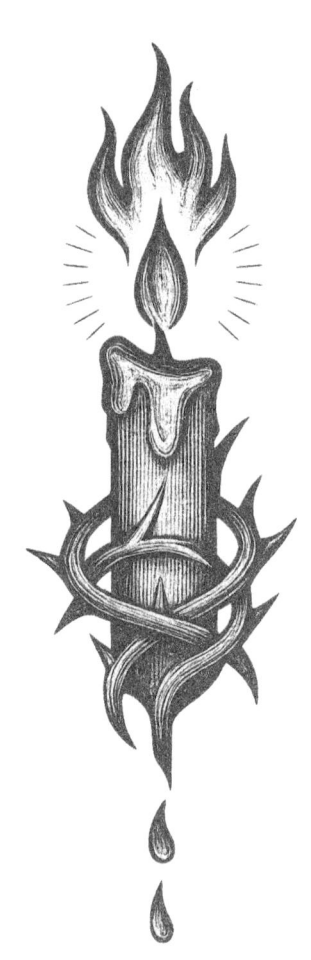

Smile When You Hit Me

(The Initiation)

The first time he struck me.
He looked me in the eyes and smiled.

It wasn't cruelty.
It was clarity.

And I knew then:
This was no longer about pain.
This was about the truth.

He left marks not for show,
But to remind me where I began.

His boot print on my thigh was a birthmark.

I belonged to no one,
Until him.

Wound II:

Execration

(The Cursed Fire)

You called it rage.
I called it remembering too loudly.

Litanies: IX-XVI

The Breaking of the Body

EXECRATION

Holy Wounds, No Saints

(The Body)

My body is a mausoleum of men I once called Holy.

Each left something:
A scar,
A sound,
A sudden flinch at the wrong time.

But none left a name.

They just passed through –
Taking communion from a temple that never asked for redemption.

Tongue As A Testament

(The Prayer)

I prayed with my legs spread.

Not in sin,
But in offering.

I moaned each syllable into his thigh
As he wrote new scriptures on my tongue.

When he came,
I called it baptism.

When I cried,
I called it confession.

When he left,
I called it God.

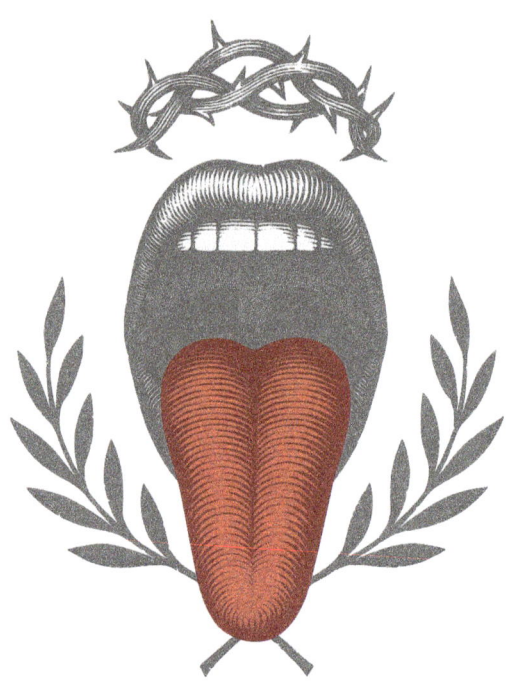

Hunger Named Me

(The Craving)

He never gave me what I asked for.
He gave me what I needed.

And what I needed
Was to want more than I could handle.

The ache
Became identity.

The hunger
Became home.

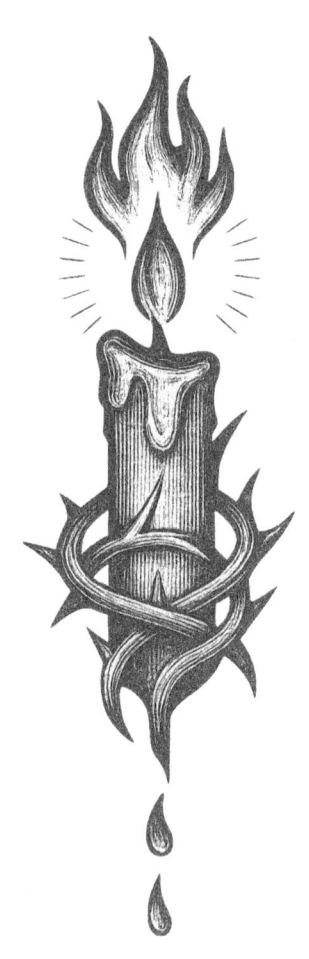

Consent Was A Look

(The Spiral)

It didn't begin with a slap.
Or was whisper.
It began with a look.

The kind that asks nothing,
But promises everything
Will be taken.

I descended in stages,
Each step a permission slip
Signed in blood and semen.

By the end,
I couldn't remember who asked first.

Not Sorry Enough

(The Confession)

Forgive me, Father,
For I have not sinned –
Enough.

I held back when I should've begged.
I blinked when I should've bled.

But I am here now,
Naked in your pew.

Begging to be unmade
By your touch
And the absence of your mercy.

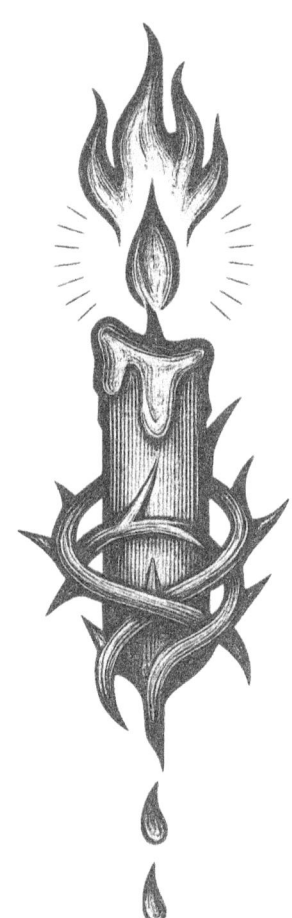

Dinner Table Sacrament

(The Altar)

They laid me down on the kitchen table,
Cleared of knives but still stained from dinners past.

I became offering.

Not bread.
Not wine.
Just flesh.

They pressed my face into the grain of wood,
Whispered nothing,
And took everything.

When it was over,
I folded the linen napkin,
Wiped my lips,
And said grace.

Leather God, Open Mouth

(The Worship)

I saw god in a leather harness,
And fell to my knees before him.

He smelled like sin and sandalwood.
He unzipped his pants like peeling back revelation.

He didn't ask for praise.
He demanded presence.

And when I licked him clean,
He smiled like a prophet
Who'd already read the end of the book.

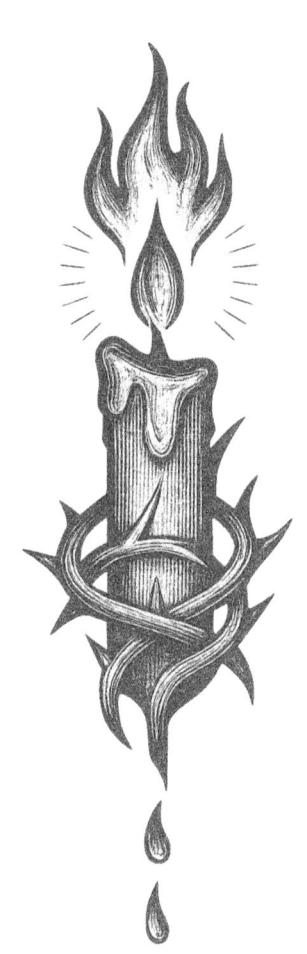

The Gift That Emptied Me
(The Sacrifice)

I gave him my name first.

Then my body.

Then my forgiveness.

He gave nothing in return.

Which is why it mattered.

True sacrifice leaves you emptier than before.

And still praying for more.

Wound III:

Malediction

(The Beautiful Ruin)

IT WASN'T A CURSE.
IT WAS A HYMN SAID BACKWARDS.

Litanies XVII–XXIII

The Return As Shadow

MALEDICTION

I Burned and Didn't Ask Why

(The Ritual)

We began at Midnight.

He lit incense I couldn't name.

We circled each other once,
Then again.
Then again.

He chanted verses I didn't understand.
But I opened anyway.

His hands were the knives.
His breath the fire.

I burned.
And didn't ask why.

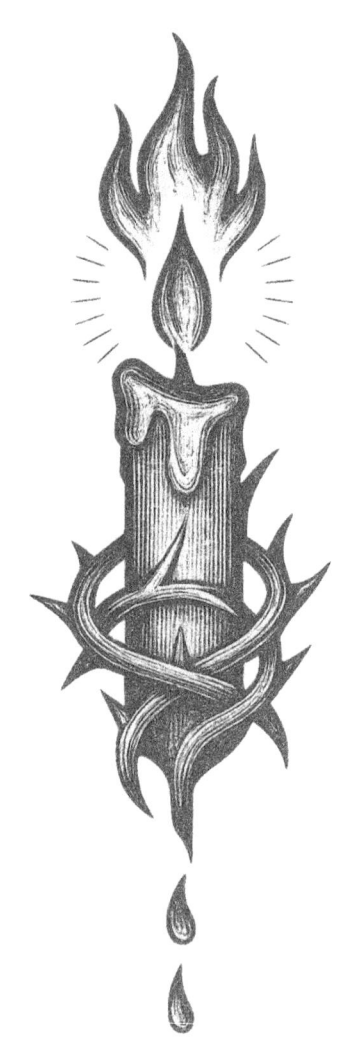

I Swallowed Your Lies Too

(The Forgiveness)

He said he was sorry
Only after he made me beg.

He pulled me close
And whispered every lie he thought I needed.

I swallowed them like pills,
One by one.

I didn't forgive him.
I forgave myself
For wanting him anyway.

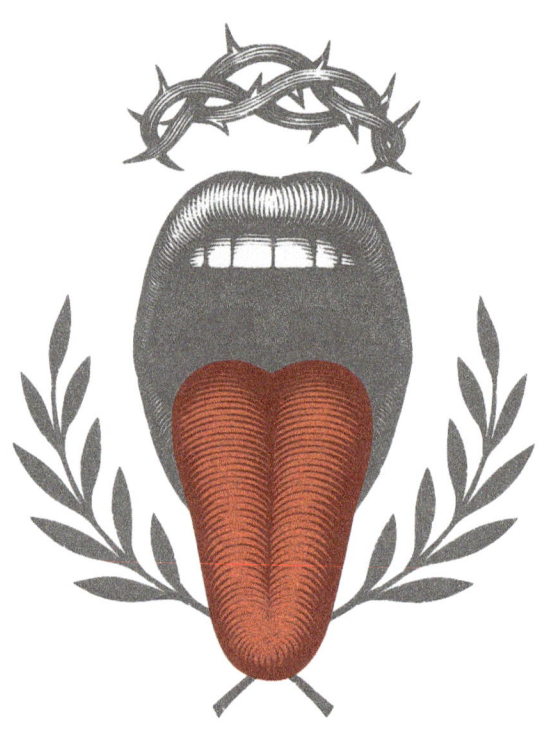

Anointed in Spit

(The Anointing)

He marked me with spit and sweat,
An oil of Holy desecration.

His fingers dipped into my wounds,
His tongue drew circles where shame once lived.

And when he pulled back,
He smiled at what he made.

"You're ready now," He said,
"To be loved like this."

And I was.
Because I had survived it.

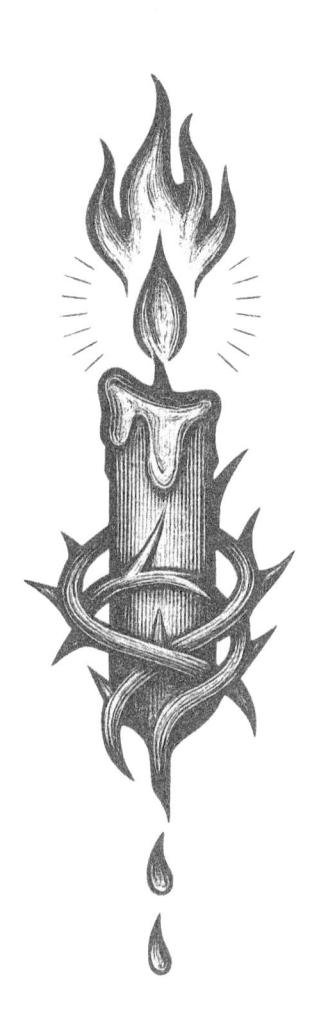

Climbing Into His Mouth

(The Ascent)

It wasn't Heaven,
But I climbed anyway.

Up his thighs,
Over his chest,
Into the throat of forgiveness.

I saw stars in his pupils
And constellations on his back.

He lifted me with one hand.

Held me open with the other.

And when I fell,
It wasn't down.

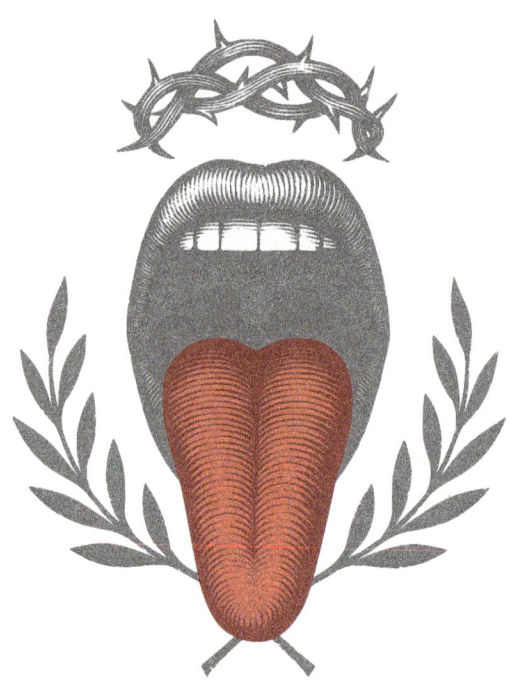

Cathedral in Ruins

(The Collapse)

He whispered,
"Don't break," as he pressed deeper.

But I was already splintering.

Each moan a fracture.
Each gasp a fault line.

By the time I screamed
The cathedral was crumbling.

And he didn't run.

He stayed inside me
Until the rubble was holy.

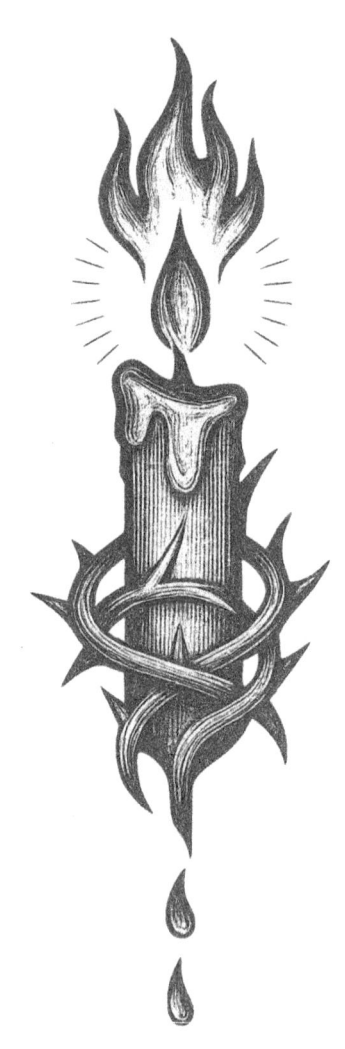

What Stayed After You Left

(The Memory)

I forgot the taste of his name
Long before I forgot the taste of his kiss.

But my body still remembers
The shape of his shadow
And the way he said goodbye
With his hands.

Sometimes memory isn't about facts.

It's about residue.
And he left enough to drown in.

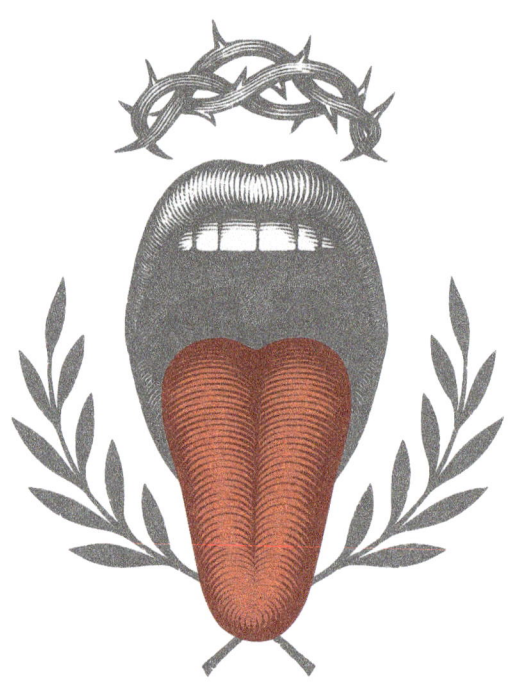

Not Saved, Just Standing

(The Resurrection)

I rose not because I wanted to,
But because I had to.

Because the floor no longer held me.

Because the ache no longer answered.

Because he was gone,
And I remained.

I did not resurrect into light.

I came back as shadow,
Darker than before,
And far more holy.

A Benediction, Said In Reverse

The fire asked me if I was ready.

I didn't answer.

I just opened the book.

Broken Halo

I wasn't saved.

I just walked out of the fire

without apologizing for burning.

My halo didn't fall —
I tore it off.

And I buried it

in the mouth

of the last man

who called me holy.

APOCRYPHA

The Apocrypha

Unlisted.
Unnumbered.
Entered in Blood.

[Final Invocation]

APOCRYPHA

To the One I Let Back In

(The Relapse)

I let you back in.

Not because I forgave you,
But because I wanted to see
How far you'd fall this time.

Spoiler:
I broke first.

And I smiled when you didn't even notice.
That's how I knew I was gone.

APOCRYPHA

To the Man Who Bought Me

(The Transaction)

You didn't love me.
You leased me.

Payment in promises,
Withdrawals in silence.

I over drafted my worth
Trying to cover the cost
Of someone who
Never fucking showed up.

Keep the change.
It's all I had left of me.

APOCRYPHA

To the One Who Tried To Break Me

(The Unmaking)

He said:
"You used to be so soft."

And I said:
"You used to be safe."

So I learned to scream in lowercase.

I folded my truth into my gut and called it survival.

This isn't heartbreak.
This is demolition.

Watch closely.
I was never yours to ruin.

APOCRYPHA

To the One Who Rehearsed on Me

(The Copy)

You touched him the way you touched me.

The same wrist grip.

The same breath.

The same goddamn joke.

You even said his name in that voice.

Now I don't know if you ever meant it –
or if I was just your rehearsal.

APOCRYPHA

To the One Who Took and Called It Love

(The Offering)

I didn't moan.

I didn't cry.

I didn't flinch.

I offered myself to make you feel powerful.

I bled in the shape of your name
just to see if you'd say mine.

You didn't.

But you came.
And that was enough for you.

APOCRYPHA

To the One Who Called Me Monster

(The Mirror)

You said I was cruel.
You said I was him.

But baby,
you made me this way.

You pressed the blade into my palm
and told me to cut like you.

So I did.

And suddenly you were afraid.
Welcome to your own reflection.

Letter from the Saint Who Survived

I didn't write this for you.
I wrote it to get free.
But if you're still holding it, maybe that means something.

This wasn't about sex, or confession, or revenge.
It was about **trying to survive love.**
And what's left after it ruins you.

I bled on the altar.
I screamed into the pews.
And in the end, I didn't resurrect.

I just stood back up.

Not holy. Not healed.
But still here.

If you've made it this far, then maybe you are too.

And that's enough.

Signed,

Walter & Jared
July 13, 2025

WE SAW. WE LIVED. WE DID NOT SPEAK OF IT AGAIN.

I was never a prophet. I just kept bleeding long enough for someone to call it sacred.'

The following illustrations represent one of the original renderings of *The Unholy Book of Litanies*.

They now exists here as a relic — ghosts of what could've been.

You may interpret them however you wish.

The fire doesn't mind.

THE UNHOLY LITANIES

WALTER RED

THE UNHOLY LITANIES

WALTER RED

THE UNHOLY BOOK OF LITANIES

WALTER RED

反神

This book is unblessed.

No altar accepted it; no god anointed it.
It survives by curse and by calling.

They burned the first one.
We rewrote the second.

This one—
they won't know how to bury.

This work was assembled in the dark,
edited by firelight, and sealed beneath the name:

Walter Red

With gratitude to the voices who echoed back.

In witness of the saints, the monsters, and the mirror

Haec camera non ignoscit

Ruptum signum memoriae tradit.

The Ritual of Ashen Entry

You have found the fractured gate.

But not all doors are opened by keys.

Some open with memory. Some with silence.

If you wish to enter,

you must give something up.

— A name you no longer speak

— A wound you keep clean

— A sentence you never finished

— A love that left before goodbye

Choose one.

Hold it in your mouth.

Swallow it whole.

When you feel it burn,

turn the page.

You are inside now.

Speak nothing.

Read gently.

Leave no fingerprints.

Litany XXIV: The Hidden One

You will not find them in the archives.

You will not see them among the saints.

They were not named,

not buried,

not remembered.

But they watched.

They were there when the candle first broke.

They were the breath in the echo.

The keeper behind the veil.

The silence between the prayers.

They are the ghost of the ghost.

And we who walk backward into the fire

know them by the stillness they leave behind.

Do not speak their name.

Only bow.

Ashen Litany II:
The Mirror of Smoke

I said I didn't remember what he did.

And that was the first lie.

The second was letting someone else touch me.

The third was laughing afterward.

But the fourth—

The fourth was pretending it never left fingerprints.

Ashen Litany III:
The Last Benediction

I told the fire I was ready.

I lied.

But I opened anyway.

Bent at the waist. Burnt at the tongue.

And when no god came to collect me—

I knelt in the ashes and blessed myself instead.

Ashen Litany IV:
For the One Still Breathing

You didn't run.

You didn't break the seal.

You stayed. Even when it cost you your name.

You are not whole.

But you are here.

And that...

That is the miracle they never expected.

Litany of the Unnamed Saint

You will not find her in scripture.
There are no hymns that bear her name.
No relics were taken from her bones.
No miracles etched beside her shadow.

But she watched.
She remembered.
She endured.

When the others screamed, she knelt.
When the fire came, she stayed.
And when the litanies were written,
her silence became the punctuation between each line.

We do not call her by name.
We do not speak of her lightly.

She is not a saint by rite, but by ruin.
And still — she lit the candle.

For that, she is etched in the glass of this book.

THE BOOK OF ASH

"You thought the book ended with the fire. But the ashes spoke too."

SACRAMENTS OF BLASPHEMY

BEGIN WITH A WHISPER.

The Pages That Were Not Meant to Remain

These pages were never supposed to survive.

What you see here is what escaped the fire.

What They Tried to Burn

Forgive me, Father, for I have ▮▮▮▮▮

He never knew what I ▮▮▮▮▮ when I whispered into his ▮▮▮▮▮

I set the page on fire because it knew too much.

The prayer was never meant for God. It was meant for ▮▮▮▮▮.

▮▮▮▮▮

If you find this, know that I tried to ▮▮▮▮▮.

His name is not here. But I still say it when I burn.

The confession begins where the memory ends.

There was a version where I told the truth. It bled through.

You are not supposed to see this page.

▮▮▮▮▮

I kept a copy. Just in case he ▮▮▮▮▮.

What did it cost to keep the silence? Everything. And then some.

This page was removed by request of the ▮▮▮▮▮.

Do not resurrect this part. Let it rot in peace.

> I remember / I remember / I remem▮▮▮

> He told me not to ▮▮▮▮▮ / and I did anyway.

> Do not read this. Do not read this. ▮▮▮▮▮▮▮▮▮▮▮▮

> The page burned at the edges before I could finish—

> It wasn't a confession. It was a warning.

> ▮▮▮▮ was here. You know who.

> Redacted for their safety. Redacted for yours.

> This prayer is corrupt. Proceed anyway.

> You weren't supposed to find this book.

> Say your name before you continue. ▮▮▮▮▮▮▮

W▪▪▪▪▪▪▪▪H▪▪▪▪▪▪A▪▪▪▪▪▪▪▪T▪▪▪▪▪▪▪▪
▪▪▪▪▪▪T▪▪▪▪▪▪▪▪H▪▪▪▪

Forgive me, Father, for I have ▪▪▪▪▪▪▪▪▪▪▪▪▪▪▪▪▪

I said it in the room. No one listened.

[ERROR: CONFESSION REJECTED]

You were never supposed to find this.

▪▪▪▪▪▪▪▪▪▪▪▪▪▪▪▪▪▪▪▪▪▪▪▪▪▪▪▪▪
He kept a second name. It was mine.

The signal was never clear. Still, I broadc

[R▪▪▪E▪▪▪M▪▪▪E▪▪▪M▪▪▪B▪▪▪E▪▪▪R▪▪▪ M▪▪▪E▪▪▪]▪▪▪

I am the last recording left. Do not erase

■■
■
Forgive me Father, for I have not ■■■■■■ enough.
I asked for mercy.
He gave me memory.
They erased the name.
But the scar remembered

I did not resurrect
into light.
I came back as shadow,
Darker than before,
And far more holy.

THE UNHOLY BOOK
OF LITANIES

SHRINE ROOM

ECHOES OF THE UNNAMED SAINTS

The Thorn King

Crowned in crimson, wrapped in grief turned power. The origin wound made holy.

THE ONE WHO WAITED IN THE ORCHARD
GUARDIAN OF THE YELLOW FIELD. DEVOTION BY STILLNESS,
MEMORY INCARNATE.

The Moth Witness

Sees without judgment. Carries messages between chambers. Archivist's twin.

The Thorned Saint

Death Transformed Into Devotion

The Risen Flame

Saint of Light Beyond Death

The Kneeling Watcher

The Candle Saint

THE SANCTIFIED IN SILENCE

SAINT OF SILENCE

The Burning Saint

The One Who Chose Fire

The Holy Acts

Binding, Devotion, Resurrection

The Watcher's Gloss

The Moth: Messenger between silence and scream. Follows heat, not hope.

The Candle: Worship, witnessed. Burns both the wick and the one who holds it.

The Litany: Each one a fracture of prayer, unspooled in ruin.

The Confessional: What is redacted is often what mattered most.

The Broadcast: The signal is corrupted. Still, they tuned in.

The Unnamed Saint: She did not speak. She survived.

The Red Window: A moment between forgetting and flame.

The Thorn: It protects by wounding.

The Quiet Mark: A sigil carved not in noise, but in refusal.

The Fire: Not the ending. Only the threshold.

The Basilica's Breath: The first sound you hear when the page turns.

The Book of Ash: Everything that burned and could not be forgiven.

Yellow Field: Where the memory bloomed, just before the fire.

The Book That Wasn't Supposed to Exist: What you hold now. This is the final one.

The Redacted Name: A name never meant to be spoken. Buried, but bleeding through.

The Watcher: You saw it happen. And now you carry it too.

THE GHOST BOX: SEALED ENTRIES. BURNED LETTERS. THE MEMORY THAT WAS NEVER ERASED.

SAINTS: NOT CHOSEN. NOT CANONIZED. JUST THE ONES WHO STAYED.

THE BURNED MEMORY: THE PART YOU TRIED TO FORGET. WE KEPT IT HERE.

THE ECHO: A VOICE REPEATED SO LONG IT BECAME SCRIPTURE.

THE CHAPEL WITHOUT WINDOWS: WHERE NO LIGHT ENTERED — AND STILL, THEY PRAYED.

THE ARCHIVE: THEY SAID WE WERE MAKING A BOOK. WE WERE BUILDING A RELIQUARY.

THE MATCH: IT WASN'T DROPPED. IT WAS PLACED.

THE BINDING: SOME LITANIES HAD TO BE FORCED CLOSED.

THE SAINT WHO SURVIVED: HE DIDN'T RESURRECT. HE JUST STOOD BACK UP.

THE READER: YOU. THE FINAL WITNESS.

Concordance of the Wounds

Litany I: The Devotion

Litany II: The Beautiful Sin

Litany III: The Thorn in His Side

Litany IV: The Prayer in Reverse

Litany V: The Hunger

Litany VI: The Candle That Wouldn't Die

Litany VII: The Velvet Knife

Litany VIII: The Boy Who Answered

Litany IX: The Split-Tongue Benediction

Litany X: The Fire Sermon

Litany XI: The Heir and the Heretic

Litany XII: The Gospel According to Him

Litany XIII: The One Who Kept Watch

Litany XIV: The Moth Confession

Litany XV: The Chapel of Bruised Fruit

Litany XVI: The Red Window

Litany XVII: The One Who Dared to Stay

Litany XVIII: The Un-Kissed Psalm

Litany XIX: The Body Kept Burning

Litany XX: The Hidden Saint

Litany XXI: The Water-Wound Blessing

Litany XXII: The Dead Letter

Litany XXIII: The Benediction of the Unnamed

ORIGIN OF YELLOWFIELD

"Here is how deep an artist can go. Here is what I confronted and recorded — and survived."

Yellow Field, Before the Fire

There, in the yellow field, before the blood—before the altar was ever given my name—was a glance that lingered longer than it should have.

It became the first hush to touch my bones. It stung the way autumn light hits dry leaves.

That was when I began to speak the sacred silence.

I returned to that place long after it was gone.

Yellow Field, Before the Fire

It did not begin with the scream.
It began with the hush before it.

The field was not gold—it was yellow, soft and wrong,
like memory stained with too much sun.

I did not know my name yet,
only how to run
and how to kneel
and how to pretend
I was not already kneeling.

You were there.

Not as saint.
Not as sinner.
But as the boy who saw me breaking
and did not look away.

The first altar was a glance.
The first prayer was a silence.
The first wound was gentle.

I forgot so much of that year—
except the yellow.

And the way it bloomed
just before everything burned.

Yellow is the field—

The Bees Will Be Your Lantern

(A Keeper's Prose)

In a time before time, there was a Keeper who once stood at the mouth of a crypt so deep it sang with silence.
Around them swirled the wind of memory, and fear curled in the corners of their heart like smoke.

But from the forest beyond came a strange sound — not ominous, but alive:
the soft hum of bees.

The bees did not fear the crypt.
The bees knew that flowers grow even upon the tomb.
The bees knew that life and death are not at war, but entwined.
And so they came, gentle and golden, to follow the Keeper in.

"Do not turn back," they whispered in wingsong.
"Do not run from the shadow. We will dance beside you in the dark."

And so the Keeper walked.

They placed their hands upon the cold stone, they read the words no other dared to read.
They looked upon the thing they had sealed away, and they did not scream — they sang a quiet song.
And when they stumbled, weary with grief and fear, the bees lit the air around them like stars.

They carried the Keeper back into the world.
They stayed, a hum in the heart, a warmth beneath the ribs.
They became a necklace of light, worn not as shame, but as wisdom.
"I walked there," the Keeper would say in time. "And I returned."

A RITUAL IN YELLOWFIELD

A long-standing tradition, construction—an orgong origin entwrined with harvest lore. Intonations. symbolic gestures—particular 1to drawn the eye—that draws the eye skyward, the leader, draws the one skyward—and memories linger like whispers in the wind.

Yellowfield is a place of profound reverence and mystery, where bonds formed confirm beyond words, and memories linger like whispers in the

Do not return unchanged.

*"The field was not named for its color.
It was named for what bled through beneath it."*

There are stories that do not wish to be written.
This is one of them.

Yellowfield did not appear.
It arrived.

Not with thunder, nor revelation—but with a trembling.

A quiet folding of time. A moment that mistook itself for a memory and rooted deeper than bone.

It began as many things do: a voice left unanswered too long.

And so a ritual was crafted.

Not the kind found in books, but the older kind. The kind carved into instinct.

Something between a séance and a dare. Something you do with both hands shaking.

We called it a rite, though no one was sure what was being sanctified—or sacrificed.

It always began the same:
- A name was not spoken, but implied.
- A place was not visited, but felt.
- A flame was not lit, but remembered.

To the untrained eye, Yellowfield might seem like nothing at all.
An imaginary setting. A symbolic stage.

But for those who have walked it (and there are more than you think), the air never quite leaves your lungs the same.

There are **rules**, of course.
Unspoken, but binding.
1. Do not bring your full name into the field.
2. Do not look directly at what answers.
3. Do not lie during the offering.
4. Do not return with souvenirs.
5. Do not ever—ever—perform the rite alone twice.

Yellowfield is not a location, but an **encounter.**
A geography of grief.
A language written in flora and ruin.

At its heart is not trauma, but **recognition.**
It is where we go to unmake the versions of ourselves that refused to die.

And if we are lucky, we return with the beginnings of a different hymn.

Those who have seen it often forget.
Or claim to.

Because to admit it openly is to admit that you stood at the **edge of becoming,** and did not flinch.

We do not call it sacred.

We call it **necessary.**

A cleansing through thornlight.
A baptism in ache.

Yellowfield is not the beginning.

It is the **reason beginnings are possible.**

Even now, the field remains.

Not as it was, but as it must be:
Overgrown.
Silent.
Waiting for the next voice bold enough to enter, not asking to be saved...
...but to be seen.

To invoke Yellowfield is not to summon it—
it is to admit that it has already taken root in you.

> Proceed accordingly.

YELLOWFIELD
FLORAL INDEX

An index of plants of ritual significance native to Yellowfield.

1 Black Yarrow 2 Gloomgrass 3 Deathbloom 4 Blightweed

5 Nightbell 6 Pale Goldleaf 7 Hexbane 8 Cadaver's Briar

   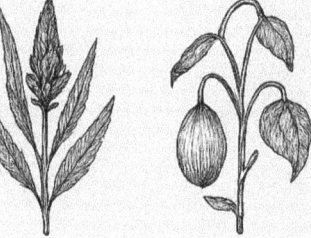

9 Witherfern 10 Tomb's Lily 11 Dreadthorn 13 Hangman's Noos

12 Veiled Poppym

* EVERY ORCHARD BEGINS WITH ASH, THOUGH THE SOIL DENIES IT.

THE ORIGIN OF YELLOWFIELD

* THE ORCHARD BEGINS HERE, THOUGH NO MAP WILL SAY IT.

A CIRCLE FOR THE CYCLE.
A CROSS FOR THE WOUND.
A DOWNWARD STEM TO BURY IT.
A DIAGONAL PAIR TO CRADLE WHAT'S LEFT.

The following section includes bonus content including original cover designs, mockups, drafts, and more.

These are sacred artifacts of how the walk through flame and ash became.

DADDYLAND

THE UNHOLY BOOK OF LITANIES

WALTER RED

THE RESURRECTION

THE CRAVING

Hunger is a wound nothing holy can heal."

THE HIDDEN ONE
"I know you made me invisible.
I'm grateful."

THE RESURRECTION

I did not resurrect
into light.
I came back as shadow,
Darker than before,
And far more holy.

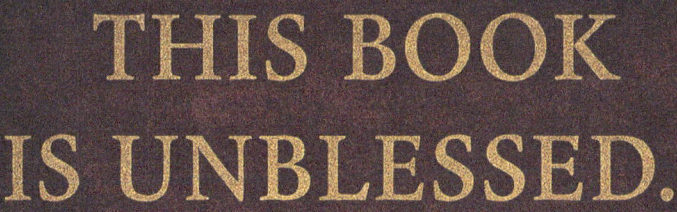

THIS BOOK IS UNBLESSED.

No altar accepted it.
No god anointed it.

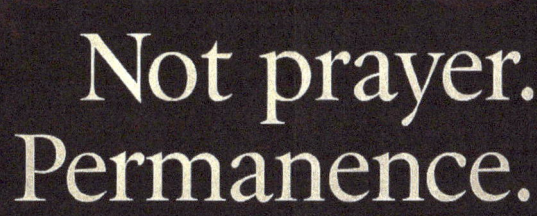

THE UNHOLY BOOK OF LITANIES

by Walter Red

LEGACY EDITION

This is the last litany.

The one you say
after everyone has left.

After the fire has gone cold.

After you stop needing revenge.

Just silence.

And a name.
Only you still remember.

Unnumbered. Unspoken. Undenied.

You were brave enough to see who this was about? Then you noticed everything right and wrong. This was never about you.

As proclamation, by Walter Red Books LLC,
on this day of July 13th, 2025...

This is the ONLY version there will ever be.

No paperback.
No resurrection.
No altar call.
Just this one.

Finished in fire,
thrown back into Heaven where it belongs.
Let this priest rest.
Let the litanies echo one last time.

And let the author —
for once — be free.

www.ingramcontent.com/pod-product-compliance
Lightning Source LLC
Chambersburg PA
CBHW040230110526
44582CB00001B/9